Morphē Arts Publications, London UK.

Morphē Arts is an independent Christian charity who offer
mentoring to recent graduates of the Creative Arts. For more
information visit www.morphearts.org

Copyright © Morphē Arts, 2017 ISBN 978-0-9957530-1-3

Bible texts from New International version, copyright Harper
Collins Christian Publishing, Nashville, usa, 2017

Morphē
Arts

SDG

ALASTAIR GORDON

BIBLE STUDIES
FOR ARTISTS

CONTENTS

1. WORK WITH ALL YOUR HEART   6
     Colossians 3:23

2. THE CREATIVITY OF GOD   10
     Genesis 1

3. THE FIRST ART COLLECTIVE   14
     Exodus 35:30-34

4. ART IDOL   18
     Exodus 32: 1-14

5. JESUS THE IMAGE OF GOD   22
     Colossians 1: 15-20

6. RESPONDING TO CULTURE   26
        Acts 17: 16-28

7. ART IN THE NEW CREATION   30
        Revelation 21: 9-21

8. FEELING WORRIED?   34
        Phil 4:4-7
        Matthew 6:25-34

9. WHAT IS SUCCESS ANYWAY?   38
        Proverbs 2: 1-11

1. WORK WITH ALL YOUR HEART

"MOST OF THE SUCCESSFUL ARTSTS IVE MET ARE VERY DISCIPLINED.
THEY TURN UP ON TIME. THEY PUT IN THE HOURS. THAT IDEA OF US
ALL BEING A BIT CHAOTIC AND SHAKY, IT'S A MYTH.
ARTISTS ARE DOERS!"
GRAYSON PERRY

1. What motivates you to work? Why do you do it and
who do you make art for?

Read Colossians 3: 23-24

*23 Whatever you do, work at it with all your heart, as
working for the Lord, not for human masters, 24 since you
know that you will receive an inheritance from the Lord as
a reward. It is the Lord Christ you are serving.*

Paul is writing to Christians in the cosmopolitan town
of Colosse. Many of the Christians had been persuaded
by hollow philosophies that seemed to undermine the
supremacy of Christ. Paul writes to encourage them to
remain rooted and built up in Jesus.

2. Who does Paul instruct the Colossian Christians to work for?

3. What does it mean to work for the Lord, not for human masters, when you also have a wider audience of critics, curators, tutors, collectors and other artists?

4. What attitude does Paul encourage the Christians in Colosse to adopt in their work? What does it mean for you to work with all your heart in your art?

5. What reward is Paul referring to in verse 24? How does this shape your motivation for working at your art with all your heart?

6. In the past Christian artists from a Reformed background used to print the initials SDG at the beginning of their books and scores of music. SDG (short hand for the Latin *Soli Deo Gloria*) meant "for the glory of God alone." Imagine these initials scribbled at the start of your sketchbook or typed on your screensaver. How might the ethos of SDG inform your daily art practice?

Father, you have instructed me to work with all my heart. Help me to understand this calling and give me the courage to honour you in every aspect of my artistic practice. Help me to honour others around me in the arts and so to honour you, the author of all creativity. Bless the work of my hands in Jesus name.

2. THE CREATIVITY OF GOD

"IT IS NO COINCIDENCE THAT THE WESTERN ATTRACTION TO SUBLIME
LANDSCAPES DEVELOPED AT PRECISELY THE MOMENT WHEN
TRADITIONAL BELIEFS IN GOD BEGAN TO WANE."
ALAIN DE BOTTON

1. Imagine God is in a crit. What would you say about his
work and creative practice?

Read Genesis 1

*1 In the beginning God created the heavens and the earth.
2 Now the earth was formless and empty, darkness was
over the surface of the deep, and the Spirit of God was
hovering over the waters.*

*3 And God said, "Let there be light," and there was light.
4 God saw that the light was good, and he separated the
light from the darkness. 5 God called the light "day," and
the darkness he called "night." And there was evening,
and there was morning—the first day.*

Right from the opening of the bible it is clear that God is for creativity. It's the first thing God chooses to tell us about Himself in His eternal word. God is creative. As those made in his image (Gen 1:27) we know that creativity is part of what it means to be human. No further justification required. In being creative we can gloriously reflect the character of God Himself.

2. How does God create? What are the similarities and differences with the way we create?

3. Genesis 1:27 tells us we are all made in the image of God. How does the way God creates make you think about your own art practice?

4. The Psalmist describes how the creation praises it's maker, "the heavens declare the glory of God, the skies proclaim the works of his hands" (Psalm 19:1). What is your response to God's creation?

5. Look over to Genesis 2:9. What does this tell us about how God much values the way things look? How does that encourage you as an artist?

6. What is the significance of God naming his creation? How does that change the way you think about putting a title on your own work?

7. As you read Genesis 1 what do you see about the order, complexity and diversity of God's creativity? How can this influence your own art practice?

God of all creativity, you are the author and giver of life. You created the universe with wonder, complexity and order. Help me to reflect your creative character in the way I work and make art. Show me how to make things that reflect your character and that bring you pleasure.

3. THE FIRST ART COLLECTIVE

"THE MOST LIBERATING THING IS BREAKING AWAY FROM THAT MYTH OF
THE ARTIST AS 'SPECIAL UNIQUE INDIVIDUAL'. THE SOLITARY KAFKA-
LIKE PERSONALITY WORKING AWAY ON THEIR OWN AND IN SUFFERING...
IT IS FAR MORE ENJOYABLE TO DISCUSS IDEAS WITH SOMEONE WHO
HAS ALSO INVESTED IN THE WORK."
DALZIEL & SCULLION

1. In what ways do you work with others in your creative
practice? How do you find working with other people?

Read Exodus 35:30-35

*30 Then Moses said to the Israelites, "See, the Lord has
chosen Bezalel son of Uri, the son of Hur, of the tribe of
Judah, 31 and he has filled him with the Spirit of God, with
wisdom, with understanding, with knowledge and with
all kinds of skills— 32 to make artistic designs for work in
gold, silver and bronze, 33 to cut and set stones, to work in
wood and to engage in all kinds of artistic crafts.*

*34 And he has given both him and Oholiab son of
Ahisamak, of the tribe of Dan, the ability to teach others.
35 He has filled them with skill to do all kinds of work as
engravers, designers, embroiderers in blue, purple and
scarlet yarn and fine linen, and weavers—all of them
skilled workers and designers.*

2. Bezalel is the first person in the bible we are told is filled with the Spirit to do a specific task, and he's an artist! According to the text, what makes Bezalel special amongst God's chosen people?

3. What 'qualifies' Bezalel as an artist? What can we learn from that for our own practice?

4. Bezalel doesn't work in isolation. What model does God give for artists to work together? What can we learn from this? Does that mean we all have to work in collaboration all the time?!

5. Consider the quality and range of materials used by the artists. Who instructs them to use such expensive materials? What can this tell us about God's pleasure in things being well made?

6. What principals can be learned from verse 34? How can you pass on what you know to others?

Father, help me to find the right materials for the job in my current art projects. Help me to be responsible with resources of time and money as gifts from you. Help me to work with those you have put around me.

4. ART IDOL

"I NEED ART LIKE I NEED GOD"
TRACEY EMIN, TITLE OF EXHIBITION AT SOUTH LONDON GALLERY, 1997

1. What do you prize above all things in your art career? If you are being honest, what things are most likely to take the place of God in your art practice?

Read Exodus 32: 1-14

1 When the people saw that Moses was so long in coming down from the mountain, they gathered around Aaron and said, "Come, make us gods who will go before us. As for this fellow Moses who brought us up out of Egypt, we don't know what has happened to him."

2 Aaron answered them, "Take off the gold earrings that your wives, your sons and your daughters are wearing, and bring them to me." 3 So all the people took off their earrings and brought them to Aaron. 4 He took what they handed him and made it into an idol cast in the shape of a calf, fashioning it with a tool. Then they said, "These are your gods, Israel, who brought you up out of Egypt."
5 When Aaron saw this, he built an altar in front of the calf and announced, "Tomorrow there will be a festival to the Lord." 6 So the next day the people rose early and sacrificed burnt offerings and presented fellowship offerings. Afterward they sat down to eat and drink and got up to indulge in revelry.
7 Then the Lord said to Moses, "Go down, because your people, whom you brought up out of Egypt, have become corrupt. 8 They have been quick to turn away from what I

commanded them and have made themselves an idol cast in the shape of a calf. They have bowed down to it and sacrificed to it and have said, 'These are your gods, Israel, who brought you up out of Egypt.'

9 "I have seen these people," the Lord said to Moses, "and they are a stiff-necked people. 10 Now leave me alone so that my anger may burn against them and that I may destroy them. Then I will make you into a great nation."

11 But Moses sought the favor of the Lord his God. "Lord," he said, "why should your anger burn against your people, whom you brought out of Egypt with great power and a mighty hand? 12 Why should the Egyptians say, 'It was with evil intent that he brought them out, to kill them in the mountains and to wipe them off the face of the earth'? Turn from your fierce anger; relent and do not bring disaster on your people. 13 Remember your servants Abraham, Isaac and Israel, to whom you swore by your own self: 'I will make your descendants as numerous as the stars in the sky and I will give your descendants all this land I promised them, and it will be their inheritance forever.'" 14 Then the Lord relented and did not bring on his people the disaster he had threatened.

Not long after Bezalel and his group had completed work for the tabernacle a crisis arises in the Israelite camp. Moses is away and communing with God on the mountain. The people panic and ask Aaron the priest to make them a god. Bad mistake. Where previously their art had given glory to God now they were using art in a way that dishonoured Him.

2. Why did the people ask Aaron to make them an idol? What function would the idol serve?

3. What materials were used for building this sculpture? How do they compare and contrast to the materials used for building the artifacts in the tabernacle in the previous study? How is this significant?

4. Aaron wasn't a trained artist like Bezalel. Why do you think he takes it on himself to make the idol, rather than commissioning the Israelite artists?

5. At the very time Moses was receiving a commandment from God for his people not to make false idols his people were building the golden calf. Why is God justified in his anger against his people? What sin lies at the heart of idolatry?

6. How are the people saved from God's wrath? How is Moses a reflection of the future role Jesus would have for his people?

7. It is clear that not all art pleases God. What idols are you in danger of honouring in your own art practice that are a substitute for worship of the true God?

God of all power and judgement, show mercy on me where I have turned to other gods that are no gods at all. Forgive me for making idols in my art where you should receive all the glory. Please help me to serve you and honour what you have done for me in Jesus.
Thank you for your grace and mercy.

5. JESUS THE IMAGE OF GOD

1. If you were trying to make a work of art as a portrait of God where would you begin?

Read Colossians 1: 15-20

15 The Son is the image of the invisible God, the firstborn over all creation. 16 For in him all things were created: things in heaven and on earth, visible and invisible, whether thrones or powers or rulers or authorities; all things have been created through him and for him. 17 He is before all things, and in him all things hold together. 18 And he is the head of the body, the church; he is the beginning and the firstborn from among the dead, so that in everything he might have the supremacy. 19 For God was pleased to have all his fullness dwell in him, 20 and through him to reconcile to himself all things, whether things on earth or things in heaven, by making peace through his blood, shed on the cross.

Back in Colosse some of the Christians has misunderstood the supreme nature of Jesus. Paul writes a character reference for Christ to affirm his divinity and status in the creation.

2. How is Jesus described in this passage? What characteristics of Jesus particularly strike you?

3. What does it mean for Jesus to be the image (icon) of the invisible God? What does it tell us about the relationship between God the Father and the Son?

4. What can we learn about the value of the image in the character of God?

5. How does Jesus function as the image of God? What can that tell us about how our own images can function?

6. What part does Jesus have in the creation of the universe? Why was it created? Who was it created for? How then should we worship Jesus?

7. In John 1 we read how Jesus is the word (logos) of God. The word was light and expelled the darkness of the world. Take a moment to reflect on Jesus as both the word and image of God. How does this shape the way you think about Jesus? What can it tell us about the relationship between word and image in art?

Father, I praise you that we can know you better simply by looking to Jesus. Please inspire my own creativity to reflect your character. Help me to rejoice in Jesus as I strive to make images that reflect in some way your glory and intentions for the world.

6. RESPONDING TO CULTURE

1. How can works of art tell us about what people think
and believe? How can they function as signs to culture?

Read Acts 17: 16-28

*16 While Paul was waiting for them in Athens, he was
greatly distressed to see that the city was full of idols.
17 So he reasoned in the synagogue with both Jews and
God-fearing Greeks, as well as in the marketplace day by
day with those who happened to be there. 18 A group of
Epicurean and Stoic philosophers began to debate with
him. Some of them asked, "What is this babbler trying
to say?" Others remarked, "He seems to be advocating
foreign gods." They said this because Paul was preaching
the good news about Jesus and the resurrection. 19
Then they took him and brought him to a meeting of the
Areopagus, where they said to him, "May we know what
this new teaching is that you are presenting? 20 You are
bringing some strange ideas to our ears, and we would like
to know what they mean." 21 (All the Athenians and the
foreigners who lived there spent their time doing nothing
but talking about and listening to the latest ideas.)*

22 Paul then stood up in the meeting of the Areopagus and said: "People of Athens! I see that in every way you are very religious. 23 For as I walked around and looked carefully at your objects of worship, I even found an altar with this inscription: to an unknown god. So you are ignorant of the very thing you worship—and this is what I am going to proclaim to you.

24 "The God who made the world and everything in it is the Lord of heaven and earth and does not live in temples built by human hands. 25 And he is not served by human hands, as if he needed anything. Rather, he himself gives everyone life and breath and everything else. 26 From one man he made all the nations, that they should inhabit the whole earth; and he marked out their appointed times in history and the boundaries of their lands. 27 God did this so that they would seek him and perhaps reach out for him and find him, though he is not far from any one of us. 28 'For in him we live and move and have our being.' As some of your own poets have said, 'We are his offspring.'

We find ourselves with Paul in Athens, a cosmopolitan capital city bustling with great music, art and theatre. Paul demonstrates an understanding of the philosophical ideas that underpinned their culture and even quotes from famous Stoic philosophers of the time. He seems to have a decent knowledge of their culture and how their art shaped their thinking.

2. What distressed Paul as he walked around Athens? What did he do about it?

3. How did the Athenians respond?

4. What similarities can you see between Athens and the culture of the creative arts today?

5. The Athenians seemed curious and open to new philosophies and ideas. How does this compare to your corner of the art world? What opportunities and challenges are there for you as a Christian? How can you respond to cultural ideas through your art?

6. How does Paul make a connection between art works in Athens to the gospel? What can we learn from his method of cultural evangelism?

7. In verse 28 Paul quotes the Cretan philosopher Epimendes and Cilician Stoic philosopher Aratus. Sometimes it can feel like we also live, move and have our being within the world of art. How can you remain distinctive for Jesus in the art world with Christian integrity?

Father, you are Lord of all creation and culture. The arts belongs to you and you can do with them as you like. Help me to live, move and have my being in you while I also work in the arts. Help me to be live and speak for Jesus in the art world with courage and integrity.

7. ART IN THE NEW CREATION

"TOMORROW BELONGS TO THOSE WHO CAN HEAR IT COMING"
DAVID BOWIE

1. If you knew what art you would be making in the future how would it effect the way you work now?

Read Revelation 21: 9-21

9 One of the seven angels who had the seven bowls full of the seven last plagues came and said to me, "Come, I will show you the bride, the wife of the Lamb." 10 And he carried me away in the Spirit to a mountain great and high, and showed me the Holy City, Jerusalem, coming down out of heaven from God. 11 It shone with the glory of God, and its brilliance was like that of a very precious jewel, like a jasper, clear as crystal. 12 It had a great, high wall with twelve gates, and with twelve angels at the gates. On the gates were written the names of the twelve tribes of Israel. 13 There were three gates on the east, three on the north, three on the south and three on the west. 14 The wall of the city had twelve foundations, and on them were the names of the twelve apostles of the Lamb.

15 The angel who talked with me had a measuring rod of gold to measure the city, its gates and its walls. 16 The city was laid out like a square, as long as it was wide. He measured the city with the rod and found it to be 12,000 stadia in length, and as wide and high as it is long. 17 The angel measured the wall using human measurement, and it was 144 cubits thick. 18 The wall was made of jasper, and the city of pure gold, as pure as glass. 19 The foundations of the city walls were decorated with every kind of precious stone. The first foundation was jasper, the second sapphire, the third agate, the fourth emerald, 20 the fifth onyx, the sixth ruby, the seventh chrysolite, the eighth beryl, the ninth topaz, the tenth turquoise, the eleventh jacinth, and the twelfth amethyst. 21 The twelve gates were twelve pearls, each gate made of a single pearl. The great street of the city was of gold, as pure as transparent glass.

There are several passages in the New Testament that speak of art God's people will make after Jesus returns. We see music (Rev 14:2,4) architecture (Isa 65:21,22; Rev 21) and new clothes (Rev 19:8) to name but a few. Here in Revelation we read about the great new city that God's people will live in full of art and precious materials. God has declared he is making everything new and the new city comes to earth dressed beautifully as a bride for her husband, Jesus.

2. Here the bride of Jesus is described as a beautiful city. What do you see as the relationship between God's people and the new holy city?

3. How is the holy city described? What images and materials particularly strike you?

4. The holy city shares a similar design to the tabernacle in Exodus. What might this tell us about the new city? What might it tell us about God's plans through the sweep of biblical history?

5. This vision of the new holy city is one of grandeur and wonder. Even the foundation stones are built with precious jewels. What expectations should it give us for life in the new city?

6. In Genesis we saw how God is deeply interested in the aesthetic dimension of his creation. Here in the new creation we see a similar desire for beauty. What encouragement can we take as art makers?

7. As you look at this vision of the future how does it change the way you live and make art today.

Father, thank you that those who know you have a great and glorious future to look forward to. Help me to live and create now in a way that reflects the new creation. May your kingdom come and your will be done in the creative arts as it is in heaven.

8. FEELING WORRIED?

"WHAT AN ARTIST WORRIES ABOUT WHEN HE PLANS HIS PICTURES,
IS SOMETHING... DIFFICULT TO PUT INTO WORDS. PERHAPS HE WOULD
SAY HE WORRIES ABOUT WHETHER HE HAS GOT IT 'RIGHT.' NOW IT IS
ONLY WHEN WE UNDERSTAND WHAT HE MEANS BY THIS MODEST LITTLE
WORD 'RIGHT' THAT WE BEGIN TO UNDERSTAND WHAT ARTISTS ARE
REALLY AFTER."
E. H. GOMBRICH

1. What most troubles you about your art and career?
How do you normally cope with moments of worry?

Read Philippians 4:4-7

*4 Rejoice in the Lord always. I will say it again: Rejoice! 5
Let your gentleness be evident to all. The Lord is near. 6
Do not be anxious about anything, but in every situation,
by prayer and petition, with thanksgiving, present
your requests to God. 7 And the peace of God, which
transcends all understanding, will guard your hearts and
your minds in Christ Jesus.*

*There can be lots of ups and downs in an art career. Most
of us suffer a little station anxiety about where our career
is going, will it be sustainable, what will people think of
the work and the old adage of can I pay the bills? Paul
offers good advice to all who worry.*

2. How can Paul say "Rejoice in the Lord always?" What reason does he give for being joyful in all situations?

3. Rejoicing in all situations doesn't mean pretending everything will be OK. How can you trust in God while also acknowledging difficult situations in your art?

4. Read verse 6 and 7 again. How does Paul encourage us to respond in times of worry? What is the promise for when we do?

Read Matthew 6:25-34

25 "Therefore I tell you, do not worry about your life, what you will eat or drink; or about your body, what you will wear. Is not life more than food, and the body more than clothes? 26 Look at the birds of the air; they do not sow or reap or store away in barns, and yet your heavenly Father feeds them. Are you not much more valuable than they? 27 Can any one of you by worrying add a single hour to your life?

28 "And why do you worry about clothes? See how the flowers of the field grow. They do not labor or spin. 29 Yet I tell you that not even Solomon in all his splendor was dressed like one of these. 30 If that is how God clothes the grass of the field, which is here today and tomorrow is thrown into the fire, will he not much more clothe you—you of little faith? 31 So do not worry, saying, 'What shall we eat?' or 'What shall we drink?' or 'What shall we wear?' 32 For the pagans run after all these things, and your heavenly Father knows that you need them. 33 But seek first his kingdom and his righteousness, and all these things will be given to you as well. 34 Therefore do not worry about tomorrow, for tomorrow will worry about itself. Each day has enough trouble of its own.

5. What reasons does Jesus give us not to worry? What should we do instead (v33)?

6. What will you do next time you are worried about your art? How do these verses help?

Father, help me to bring my worries to you. Show me more about your character and plans for my life that I can trust you and not stress about things that you are in control over. Please help work towards a career in art that is consistent and sustainable. Open opportunities for me and help me to trust in you whether I have a busy art schedule or nothing in the diary at all.

9. WHAT IS SUCCESS ANYWAY?

IN MOST CASES SUCCESS EQUALS PRISON... AN ARTIST SHOULD NEVER
BE: PRISONER OF HIMSELF, PRISONER OF A MANNER, PRISONER OF A
REPUTATION, PRISONER OF SUCCESS
HENRI MATISSE

1. What would success look like to you in your art? How
do you know when you've got it? How often do you think
about it?

Read Proverbs 2: 1-11

1

My son, if you accept my words
* and store up my commands within you,*

2

turning your ear to wisdom
* and applying your heart to understanding—*

3

indeed, if you call out for insight
* and cry aloud for understanding,*

4

and if you look for it as for silver
* and search for it as for hidden treasure,*

5

then you will understand the fear of the Lord
* and find the knowledge of God.*

6

For the Lord gives wisdom;
* from his mouth come knowledge and understanding.*

7

He holds success in store for the upright,
* he is a shield to those whose walk is blameless,*

8

for he guards the course of the just
* and protects the way of his faithful ones.*

9

Then you will understand what is right and just
* and fair—every good path.*

10

For wisdom will enter your heart,
* and knowledge will be pleasant to your soul.*

11

Discretion will protect you,
* and understanding will guard you.*

2. What values does the writer of Proverbs place most highly in the life of someone who follows God? How are they attained?

3. According to verse 7 where does success come from? Who is in control of it?

4. Look at verse 9. According to the proverb how do we know what is right and just? How do we get wisdom?

5. What matters most in the life of a Christian? How do matters of integrity and godliness fit into your art practice?

6. What do these verses encourage you to pray about in your art practice and how you live your life?

Father, thank you for your promise to give wisdom to all who ask for it. Help me to be wise in the way I make art and honour those around me. Let my yes be yes and my no be no. I pray that you would open doors of opportunity for my art and help me to seek first your kingdom as I try to work in a way that honours you.